THE JOURNEY TO NOW

A Discipline of Becoming

CONRAD WALLACE

ISBN: 979-8-89228-946-7   (Paperback)
ISBN: 979-8-89228-947-4   (eBook)

Printed in the United States of America

CONTENTS

There was a boy who lived in Jamaica's rural countryside, in a place called Leveldon. He lived on a farm with his grandparents, where the amenities did not include electricity or running water. When the sun went down, he relied on a lamp or a torch for light, and each day he traveled to the river to fetch water.

At the age of nine, his parents got divorced, placing an even greater strain on his navigation through life. Still, that did not prevent him from excelling in school, nor did it diminish his belief that life itself was a classroom, rich with lessons waiting to be learned.

He was sharp in his studies, often reading late into the night by the faint glow of his lamp, determined not to let darkness dictate his limits.

At twelve, his grandfather passed away, and soon after, he moved to the big city. The change was daunting, but beneath the uncertainty, a spark of excitement burned bright—this was another beginning, a new opportunity to learn even more.

He enrolled in a prominent high school and was suddenly exposed to a completely different way of life. Now he could watch television and had running water, he marveled. Although he couldn't always participate in conversations about the latest TV shows, he made friends nonetheless. From these peers, he learned many things—not all of which were beneficial for his development.

The new environment had an unfamiliar effect on the boy. Over time, his grades began to decline. However, he now lived with a very stern mother, a firm believer in education, focus, and achievement—a mother who, like him, had come from the same farm in Leveldon.

Slowly, he began to turn things around as he prepared for his final exams—the tests that would determine whether he could advance to a higher level of education.

When the exam results came back, he passed—but not with scores high enough to attend his preferred institution.

It was time to refocus and decide what would come next. The boy dreamed of becoming a pilot. But when he called the aviation school, he realized he couldn't afford the fees.

Determined, he searched for another way to achieve his dream and discovered that the Army offered a route to becoming a pilot.

He began additional studies to qualify for the officer program. Then the day came when he received a call inviting him to take the commissioned officer test. It wasn't easy. Multiple medical checks followed, and he persevered.

The day of the written test arrived. With confidence, the boy advanced through each stage:

Situational awareness—pass.

Impromptu speech—pass.

Calculation and navigation — pass.

Almost at the finish line, he felt confident that he would succeed. The final hurdle was the physical test, and he was an exceptional athlete. He gave it everything he had, pushing through each challenge until the day came for the results to be announced.

Heart pounding, he entered the room to hear his fate.

The outcome:

"Unfortunately, you did not make it."

He began the long, reflective journey home to tell his mother the news. When he arrived, he recounted the events of the day.

Now he had to ask himself: What comes next?

After some thought, he made a decision: If he couldn't join as an officer, he would enlist as a regular soldier and work his way up.

When that day arrived, with determination in his heart, he began another journey.

During military training, he remained laser-focused. He aced both the written and physical tests and advanced to graduation.

On graduation day, the boy was honored as one of the two best recruits, recognized as the most well-rounded trainee who excelled in every area.

Soon after becoming a soldier, he was selected for an advanced course because of his potential. Once again, he shone— graduating at the top of his class, commanding the parade, and receiving two awards for best student and academic excellence.

He was then promoted, becoming one of the youngest noncommissioned officers in his unit. Later, he was appointed Supervisor of Arms, a position rarely given to someone so junior, but his dedication and leadership made him the right choice.

After six years in the military, he realized that his dream of becoming a pilot could not be achieved through that path, given the structure of the institution. He decided to migrate to the United States, where his partner was living, and begin another journey.

There, he pursued his education in financial studies and excelled, eventually earning his degree. After graduation, he secured a position in a prominent organization and once again distinguished himself, rising to become a financial planning and analysis manager.

One day, as he looked out over the vast skyline of Manhattan from his office window, he reflected:

A boy from the countryside in this big city. How many people would have taken this journey? How many would have given up because the odds seemed too small?

He thought about those who had dreams but stopped trying after setbacks—those who never realized that the odds, no matter how small, still exist.

I am that boy, and on that day, I decided to write *The Journey to Now*.

There are moments when life feels like a heavy silence,
the world's weight presses on our shoulders,
and the echoes of our doubt ring louder than any hope.
In those moments, we can forget what we are truly made of,
but it is also in this struggle that we remember.

I've stood where you stand,
lost in the shadows,
wondering if the pieces of me had scattered forever.
But here's the truth: Those pieces didn't vanish—
they transformed,
shaping something new,
something stronger.

This book is not a map to find yourself.
It's a mirror to show you who you've always been.
It's a testament to the resilience that rises
from the cracks of brokenness,
a celebration of how we rebuild with every fall.

The poems within these pages are not just words—they are steps.
Each line is a choice to persevere.
Each verse is a reminder that transformation is not a destination,
but a journey we choose to walk,
one uncertain step at a time.

In these pages, you will find the strength to rise,
the courage to reflect,
and the power to redefine your purpose.
Resilience is not the absence of struggle,
but the grace we find in the process of becoming.

So I invite you to open these pages.
Let the rhythm of each poem remind you that you are not
alone.

Your journey is shared,
your strength is real,
and the transformation that awaits you is already unfolding.

This is your story,
a tale of becoming,
of choosing to rise,
again,
and again.

1 THE ART OF RISING

I wrote this during a time when life felt like one long storm—unannounced, unmerciful, and unwilling to wait for me to be ready. As a new parent, my daughter had just been diagnosed with autism, my marriage was strained, and work carried demands I was unsure how to meet. I remember standing in my kitchen one night, hands braced against the counter, feeling as though everything I'd built was slipping through my fingers. Yet even in that moment, something small inside me refused to die. This poem was born out of that sliver of defiance—proof that even when life shakes us, we are not finished.

BATTLEFIELDS

The storm arrived
Unannounced and unkind.
It did not ask permission
It tore through me
Ripping away the courage I had stitched together

But even as I trembled
Even as fear wrapped itself around me
I held on to the small bold fire still burning within

Have you ever had a period when every day felt like rain? Not the gentle kind, but the cold, inconvenient kind that catches you without an umbrella and soaks into your clothes and your spirit. I have been there.

At first, I tried to run from it, believing that struggle was a sign of failure. Eventually, I stopped avoiding it and stood still. I let the rain soak me. I learned that storms teach strength in ways that sunshine never could.

STRENGTH IN THE RAIN

Over time
I stopped fearing the rain.
I let it soak into my skin.
I stood in the storm
And fought for the light,
Even as the shadows
Tried to swallow me whole.

Each fall left me with something new—
A lesson,
A scar,
A spark of strength that refused to let me surrender.

The battles were never random.
They came to shape me,
To carve me into the person I was always meant to be.

The story of Colonel Sanders has always amazed me. It's one I return to often—not because of his success, but because of his persistence. By sixty, he had endured failure after failure: a business lost to fire, another undone by a new highway. Yet at sixty-five, armed with nothing more than a recipe and an unshaken belief, he chose to try again. His life reminds us that persistence is its own form of victory—a lesson every classroom, every person, can hold onto. Late does not mean the end. It simply means you keep going.

BEING

The one who thinks it's not too late to be,
He will always be the one who becomes.
When the band takes flight and the song is done,
He's still relentlessly beating his drums.

And when you think his fire is snuffed out,
With his dying breath, he will fan the flame.
Disregarding the onlooker's judgment,
He is unafraid of slander or shame.

Though the world's approval may seem distant,
He does not shun what the world has to give.
And though he knows the surest gift is death,
Before this gift is bestowed, he must live.

For once life exists, being is a must.
To fear the path may leave your hopes a wreck.
It takes a mammoth's effort to endure,
Yet triumphs shine through every single speck.

I have known fear that doesn't shout—the kind that lives in the mind, whispering quietly until it becomes a language of its own. Fear once convinced me to put down my pen, to doubt my potential before I had even tried. This poem marks the moment I realized that fear and safety are not the same thing. Growth requires movement—even when our knees and hands shake.

BREAK FREE FROM FEAR

There is no life more suffocating than one lived in fear.

It presses against my chest,
steals the air from my dreams,
and crushes my potential
before it even has a chance to breathe.

I want to step forward, to begin again,
but voices, like chains, prevent these capable hands;
they whisper, "Why should you?"

This poem is small because sometimes wisdom arrives simply. I wrote it after a setback that bruised my confidence.

My failed attempt to enlist in the army as a commissioned officer was a particularly difficult moment, especially given how much I had prepared for it.

I wrote this to remind myself that effort is a form of victory, and standing up matters more than perfection.

TRY

Stand tall, rise again.
Success blooms from effort's root.
Fall but never stay.

I wrote this to honor the quiet victories—the ones that rarely make headlines but change us entirely. When I stopped being fear lead, it became a kind of superpower, unlocking every success that followed. *What is the worst that can happen if I give it a try?* This piece grew out from the realization that the world often applauds the triumph but rarely sees the trembling that precedes it.

THE ART OF RISING

When I rise above it all,
my story will not be silenced.
It will be the story
of a dreamer who dared,
a soul who refused to shrink,
a heart that chose boldness
over fear.

Usain Bolt once shared that when he lost at the Jamaican trials, he took it personally—not in ego, but in hunger. After that loss, he trained until his body rebelled, until the grass beneath his spikes held pieces of him: sweat, effort, fragments of breath. He ran again and again, stomach churning, sometimes vomiting from the strain. And still he returned the next day. And the next.

Long before the world cheered him, he lived countless unseen moments: tying his laces with tired hands, leaning over track railings to catch his breath, whispering to himself that he could be more.

His story reminded me that greatness is forged in these small, private battles—in mornings when the alarm feels like a weight, in evenings spent working when others rest, in the ache that refuses to accept average. Discipline carries the body and mind to places that talent alone cannot reach. Success is not the moment of victory; it is every moment that led there.

MOMENTS

the first alarm that pulled you from sleep
the burn in your muscles on the last repetition
the silence of staying behind to do more
the nights you sacrificed to keep going
the injury that tried to break you
the ache of pushing past limits
the plan that fell apart
only to be built again
the hours spent practicing alone

it all comes rushing back now
because it was always for this moment

and if you have no such memories
do not wonder why success feels distant
someone else carries them
etched into their bones
and they deserve it more

One of the moments I am most proud of didn't happen in a room of applause or accomplishment. It happened on a sidewalk, in the quick, sharp sting of a word that wasn't meant to describe me, but to diminish me. I remember the tone more than the syllable—the way it was hurled like a stone, loud enough for others to hear, loud enough to demand reaction. "You f—— Ninja!" For half a second, a strange feeling rose hot in my chest…and then something else arrived: calm—surprising even to me for an instant.

I smiled. I lifted my hand and waved, as I would to a neighbor rather than a stranger trying to bruise me. The person shouting only grew more frustrated, unsure what to do with a response that refused to mirror her intention. And there, while my pulse still thudded through my ribs, I had a quiet realization: We are a species still growing up. Still learning. Still fumbling toward empathy.

Later someone said, "You handled that way better than I would have. Kudos to you." In that remark—in the soft respect in their voice—I saw something good. Not perfection. Not a fixed world. But possibility. It struck me that a single gentle reaction can open a crack of light in another person's understanding.

That day reminded me that strength is not always loud. Sometimes it is simply choosing grace when harm invites you to do otherwise. Sometimes hope looks like a wave—steady, small, but undeniable.

THE THINGS I SEE

If you could see what I see—
you would see hope
pulled from the grip of despair,
fingers bruised but still holding on.

It clings to the light,
refusing to fade,
choosing courage over surrender.

HAPPINESS

even in winter, happiness drifts in like a snowflake.
unexpected, never promised, but still finding its way.

it does not wait for perfection.
it lands where it chooses,
in moments we least expect
but need the most.

and when it comes,
it wraps around us,
turning even the coldest days
into something beautiful.

My grandfather, a great man, died at the age of eighty-eight, but left me a profound gift. He once told me that the heaviest weight that a person carries is not age or failure—it is the dream they never attempted. I remember him sitting on a wall in his final years, light from the sunset catching the veins in his hands like rivers leading somewhere unfinished. He spoke softly, as if words themselves required energy he could barely spare, and he confessed that there were things he wished he had pursued while he still had the legs to chase them.

On that evening, I learned something I have never forgotten:

Regret does not appear in the early chapters of our lives; it waits until we pause long enough to notice it.

Sometimes, all it takes is stillness for the debt to speak.

This poem was born from that moment—

From the realization that the time to move is now, while breath still fills us and footsteps are ours to command.

UNPAID DEBTS

I have lived three score and then ten
And never did I feel regret
until I lay still. That was when.
I knew a debt remained unmet.

And as I lay, my regrets loomed,
My dreams, like crows, circling high,
Yet I let these fleeting sorrows fade,
Like shadows cast across the sky.

I've never left debts unpaid.
So I must no longer lie still,
But let these fleeting sorrows fade,
And face the weight of my pending bill.

Since rest is the one thing sure,
I will not help it to find me.
I'll stand erect and strive once more,
To free my soul of regret's debris.

From a countryside farm to New York City, the journey was daunting at times. I once sat in an NYC lobby waiting to be called into an interview I had rehearsed for, prayed for, and dreamed about. My resume felt too thin in my hands, and the room was too quiet—the kind of quiet where you can hear your own pulse tapping against your ribs. The kind that makes bowel movement and sweaty armpits feel like constants. When the receptionist called my name, for a second, my legs forgot they were made for standing.

I could have turned back.
I could have told myself, *Not today.*

But something more potent than fear rose in me;
a reminder of every late night I spent preparing,
every hesitation I pushed through,
every step that led me to this door.

So I stood, smoothed the tremor from my breath,
and walked toward opportunity like I was someone
who belonged there.

Not without nerves, but with refusal to be ruled by them.

That moment taught me this:
Readiness is not the absence of fear;
it is stepping forward while fear watches.

READY

Like a deer in headlights,
I am caught in the moment,
but fear will not hold me still.

This is what I have been waiting for,
the chance to rise,
to become more than I was before.

The lights are blinding
but I do not shrink.
I let them illuminate me
as I step forward
unafraid

People often ask why I'm always studying, reading, learning something new; why I never turn away from a difficult conversation or honest piece of criticism. The truth is simple: I never want to meet opportunity unprepared.

I have lived many lives: personal trainer, nutritionist, writer, finance manager, soldier, entrepreneur.

Some call it scattered; some call it unfocused.

But I have never believed that growth must travel in a straight line.

There is a quote people often repeat:

"A jack of all trades is a master of none."
But they leave out the second half:
"but often better than a master of one."

I learn because knowledge sharpens me.

I stretch myself across disciplines because each one prepares me for a door I cannot yet see.

Strength taught me discipline.
Nutrition taught me fuel and balance.
Writing taught me voice.
Finance taught me order and precision.
The military taught me endurance under pressure.
Entrepreneurship taught me to bet on myself.

Every skill is a seed.
Every study is a root.

I never want to stand before my life wishing I had done more.

So I prepare—continuously, relentlessly—because when the moment arises, I will not be scrambling; I will be ready.

The successful one will see their dreams, and like a lion lying in wait, they will ambush this chance with a vice-like grip. Without letting go, a dream will be plucked from potential into being. This must be the attitude on the journey to success; it all starts with preparation. If one is prepared, they do not back down when the chance arises. They do not leave it for tomorrow.

THE READINESS OF FLOWERS

On shattered pavement there lay a crack
From which the one flower emerged daring:
Reward hard-won, by breaking from the pack
To greet the day for which it was preparing.

This day is grasped, its promise fresh as dew.
For this day, the flower was always primed.
It watched with hope for the opportune clue
Where time, patience, and reward are aligned.

Reaching out, assured—it buds, then sprouts,
And clenches the air and sunrays with delight.
For this is a day that silenced all doubts,
A day when effort met chance in full flight.

And though the weight of waiting had been heavy,
When the crack appeared, the flower stood ready.

There was a time in my life when I could not trust my own mind.

Depression arrived quietly at first, like fog slipping under a door, then one morning I woke up and couldn't find myself in the room.

I carried anxiety in my chest like a second heartbeat, too loud to ignore, too constant to escape.

People saw me moving—smiling even—but inside I dragged a weight no one could see.

Some days, even getting out of bed felt like climbing a mountain with no summit in sight.

I avoided mirrors—they reflected someone I didn't recognize, someone small, afraid, frayed at the edges.

I didn't want to tell anyone.

Part of me believed silence was strength,

that admitting pain would make it real—irreversible.

But the truth is, speaking it was what saved me.

The first time I said aloud, "I'm not okay,"
my voice shook, yet something inside me shifted.
It was as if opening my mouth had opened a window,
and for the first time in months, air moved through me.
Not relief—not yet,
but possibility.

Healing did not arrive in a rush.
It came slowly, like light at the edge of a curtain.
One honest conversation.
One deeper breath.
One step I didn't think I could take,
but I did anyway.

I learned that pain does not vanish when we hide it.
Shame thrives in darkness.
But when we name what hurts,
we loosen its grip.

This poem reminds me of that time—
of the climb back into myself,
of the moment truth became a torch instead of a weight.

BURDENS UNKNOWN

Hushed is the tale of the bearer's burden,
One etched by an emissary's wanting.
Whichever choice is made, doom seems certain.
Screams gone past are consistently haunting.

Yet here she stands with unyielding credence,
Treading uphill on the trails of chagrin:
A road now paved with shame and achievements,
But that is where refinement will begin.

Oh, the taste of savory blissfulness looms.
It reaches out, but far in the distance,
And teasingly leaves just room to presume
Expectant thrills for actual existence.

Until this moment, her story lay fated
To find the ears where truth is reinstated.

"Conrad, you exude confidence!" This was the statement
from a former coworker. While that is true today, this was
not always the case. There were nights when the world slept,
and I could not.

I lay in the dark with only my thoughts awake.
Thoughts ran like frightened animals—
fast, uncatchable, impossible to quiet.

The room was still, yet my heart raced,
as if danger lived not outside my door
but inside my skull.
Every memory felt sharper at night.
Every regret echoed deeper.
Every fear crept closer to my bed.

I learned that anxiety has a voice,
speaking loudest when the lights go out.

Some nights I prayed sleep would find me.
Other nights I simply endured,
watching shadows stretch across the walls,
telling myself morning would come,
even if it felt like it never would.

But slowly, I discovered,
even the darkest mind must eventually unclench.
Even the loudest fear loses its grip when dawn begins to bloom.
The sun does not negotiate with the night.
It replaces it.

This poem is for those who lie awake,
who battle thoughts that run without mercy,
who search for peace in rooms where quiet offers no comfort.

There is a dawn after the longest night.
And when it comes, even anxiety must bow to the light.

SCARY NIGHTS

Through the cracks, I saw a hasty retreat.
And one went swiftly by my hiding place.
This will surely end bittersweet
With sorrow for the loser of the race.

Yet this is not the path my mind will take.
For such grim tales would keep my soul awake.

The tale of a race creaking to a halt,
With falls and bruises and no clear winner:
Only tears and losses had by default.
Tears of the righteous, tears of the sinner.

Soaking a field that would constantly take.
You wish it were a dream, and soon you'd awake.

In a place settled by those who endured,
Having no ruckus in the silent night
Where there is sleep and sweet dreams are assured
And great hope embraces the dawning of light.

There is such peace, a journey I must take,
To greet the dawn where new hopes will awake.

As I move through life, I meet people carrying their own battles. My journey has taught me to share my story of overcoming—not as proof that pain disappears, but as evidence that healing is possible. Many of the stories I've heard made me realize that there are places where dreams can be achieved, yet in this dreamland, many dreams are also shredded. One woman's experience remains vivid years after she shared it—years of physical and emotional abuse, years surviving what was meant to shatter her.

One day, she shared that she felt ruined, as if the damage might define her forever. The moment of questioning had arrived
And I shared with her what I knew to be true:

"The fact that you are still here means you are still winning."
Survival is victory.
Protection is victory.
Choosing a better future, even through pain, is victory.

She did not walk away weak.
She walked away powerful.
Not because she carried no scars,
but because she understood she must refuse to let those scars stop her
from building something better—both for herself
and for the child who now walks beside her.

This poem is for her.
For those sometimes perceived as the most fragile, yet who keep defying the odds time and again. For every woman who was meant to break, but rose anyway—trembling, radiant, victorious.

VICTOR

She ran her hands across her face.
A reminder: She remained in this place.
The scars she bore were proof of battles won,
A warrior's resolve under every sun.

She stood, her spirit unyieldingly alight,
Fueled by memories of each past fight.
The weight of challenges could not deter,
For every trial had been conquered by her.

And as a victor, she stood once again,
Her courage a beacon, her strength her refrain.

As a personal trainer, I've seen people walk into gyms expecting transformation in a week—stronger bodies, clearer minds, better lives. But real change doesn't arrive quickly. It arrives quietly—rep by rep, choice by choice, day after day.

I've watched clients start with five-pound weights and trembling hands, with fifteen-minute walks instead of full workouts, with small meals prepared intentionally, instead of whatever was easiest.

Those moments never look heroic to the onlooker,
yet they are victories all the same.
Strength is not built in one grand effort.
It is built through continuation.

Real breakthroughs happen when someone shows up again,
even when tired, even when discouraged,
even when progress feels invisible.

That is growth—not in leaps, but in inches.

This is for every athlete, every client, every human
who lay down in exhaustion but sprouted anyway,
who kept pushing forward through soreness, doubt, or pain.
Consistency is the flame that keeps us alive—moving,
evolving. We grow because we continue.

CONTINUATION

I lie down
Yet I sprout

Fueled by the essence of life's quiet flame

I am wounded, yet
Growth endures

Let me take you back to the countryside of Jamaica, where I grew up.

Life there began before the sun was fully awake. I'd step outside to the sound of roosters calling the morning into being, carrying feed for the chickens and goats before getting ready for school. There was no electricity then—only the steady glow of a kerosene lamp to study by at night, its flicker dancing across my notebooks as I tried to absorb every lesson.

After the morning chores, I'd walk miles along quiet, winding roads just to reach a spot where transport might pass. Some days felt long before the school day even began. But my focus never wavered. I knew where I wanted to go, and I knew I had to push through whatever stood in my path.

Growing up like that could have made anyone waver.

But I learned early that if the goal stays clear, no challenge is too great to overcome. You must back yourself. When obstacles rise, you must find a way around them—always moving forward, always keeping the vision alive.

This poem is rooted in that truth:
No matter how murky the waters get,
with focus and determination, you will remain afloat.

MURKY WATERS

These murky waters carry a story,
Yet I refuse to let all this sorrow
Steal my crown or strip away my glory,
Nor dictate the path of my tomorrow.

Such waters will not define what I choose.
And surely, they won't serve as my excuse
To falter, to surrender, or to lose—
A prospect so grand the world can't refuse.

These waters are muddy, yet I'm a boat,
Harnessing currents to rise with the streams.
Ensuring with each row, I stay afloat
No matter how harsh or torrid it seems.

And until I escape this wretched tale,
I'll keep my grip firm; my paddles won't fail.

People love to say, "It will get better."
They say it in passing, as a reflex,
the way you might say "bless you" after a sneeze.
Sometimes it feels less like comfort, more like a script,
something people offer because silence feels uncomfortable.

I used to hear those words and feel nothing.
Better? When? How?
But life has a way of teaching quietly, slowly,
almost without your permission.

Over the years, I watched myself change—
my thoughts, my habits, the ways I responded to pain.
I grew out of old mindsets
and stepped into new versions of myself
I didn't even know I was capable of becoming.
Age changed me.
Experience shaped me.
Mistakes carved wisdom into places where doubt once lived.

Even the seasons outside my window shifted,
flowers blooming where cold earth had once hardened,
rain falling on fields cracked just weeks before.
Nothing stayed the same.
Nothing could stay the same.

So now, when life hits hard,
I don't cling to that empty phrase people repeat without thinking.
Instead, I remind myself of what I've seen,
what I've lived:

Change is constant.
Hurt is temporary.
No moment—no matter how heavy—lasts forever.

Even when it feels unbearable,
even when time moves painfully slowly,
life is already shifting beneath the surface.
What feels impossible today
will not feel the same tomorrow.

You don't have to believe everything improves instantly.
But you can trust this:

Nothing stays as it is.
Not you.
Not your circumstances.
Not your pain.

And that alone is a reason,
a real, grounded reason,
to hold on.

HOLD ON

After winter, blossoms always break through the frost.
After the night, dawn gently reveals what was lost.
After the storm, the skies clear, but they feel so empty.
After the drought, rain falls, though it doesn't heal completely.

It's just how time moves, I suppose.

So I tell myself to hold on, even when it's hard to stay.
The darkness can't last forever…or so they say.

In 1954, a young medical student named Roger Bannister stood on a track in Oxford, preparing to attempt what the world called impossible.

For decades, athletes had tried—and failed—to run a mile in under four minutes.

Doctors claimed the human body simply could not handle it.

Commentators called it a physical wall.

Scientists warned the heart would "burst under the strain."

The world repeated it so often that most runners accepted it as fact.

But Bannister didn't.
He trained between university lectures,
timing himself with a worn-out stopwatch,
and refused to let the voices of doubt decide his limits.

On May 6, 1954, he broke the barrier,
3 minutes, 59.4 seconds.

The moment he crossed the finish line,
he didn't just change his own story,
he proved that the "impossible" often collapses
the moment someone stops believing it.

Within forty-six days, another runner had broken the record.
By the following year, several more had done it.
The barrier was never physical.
It was mental.

Bannister reminded the world of something powerful:
Doubt from others can only define you
if you allow it to.
Strength begins where self-belief refuses to bend.

This poem rises from that same conviction,
that the greatest breakthroughs happen
when you take command of your mind
and refuse to surrender your limits to anyone.

CONTROL

When they say, "You're not strong enough—you'll fail,"
Stand firm and rise; let your courage prevail.
When they insist, "You cannot achieve this,"
Pursue your goal; make their doubts meaningless.

When voices urge you, "Just give up—let go,"
Work harder still and let your determination show.
For only you command your mind and soul,
So take the reins firmly; take full control.

What I Learned in Haiti About Endurance

One of my most memorable missions as a soldier was my deployment following the 2010 Haiti earthquake. When I arrived in Haiti as part of the first wave of soldiers to step onto that broken ground, I saw devastation that carved itself into memory.

Bodies were carried through streets where homes had once stood.

Families searched for water, only to find none.

Children sharing handfuls of food that could never be enough.

People were mentally and physically exhausted, grieving,
stripped of every comfort—yet somehow still standing.

They did not look fearless.
They did not look triumphant.
They looked alive, and in that landscape,
That alone was its own kind of victory.

In the middle of ruin, I learned something I have carried
ever since:
Survival is not always strength at its loudest.
Sometimes it is simply the refusal to fall,
the quiet miracle of breath after everything around you
collapses.

This poem comes from that memory,
that being here, even tired,
even shaken, is proof that we all carry a kind of resilience.

UNBREAKABLE

It's over, and you're still here.
The weight of it all should have crushed you, but it didn't.
You don't feel victorious, just tired.
Maybe that's enough—
Perhaps that's what survival looks like.

RISE

I will keep standing
even on shattered ground.

I lift my head high
Though weights pull me forward,
still I do not break.

TAKEN

You thought you broke me—left me empty, left me weak.
But the weight of your words was never mine to carry.
I wake up stronger now—lighter, freer.
You're gone, and for the first time, I see myself.
I was never the one who needed saving.

Let me take you back to my time served in the military—an unforgettable moment, one that reminds me that hope, no matter how slender, is worth clinging to.

For my team and me, hope felt like a luxury we could no longer afford. We were pinned down, low to the dirt, every breath sharp with the scent of sand and sweat—and something even darker lurked: fear. The enemy had the upper hand—we knew it. Orders were whispers; prayers were silent. For a moment, submission felt like an outcome worth considering. A moment where the world shrinks: just the pulse in your ears, the weight of your weapon, the brother beside you, hands shaking, eyes wide with uncertainty.

Yet even in that shrinking world, something held—not bravado, not blind courage. Training—the muscle memory of every drill, every long run, every shouted command. Trust in each other, in the mission, in the belief that falling didn't mean the end. Adrenaline surged like fire through our veins; though the odds were small, belief was larger. We rose. We pushed. We acted—not because certainty was promised, but because surrender wasn't a story we were willing to leave behind. And against what logic predicted, we overcame. We stood where moments earlier we had crawled. We walked away not untouched, but undefeated.

This poem is for that version of us—the one who trembles but moves forward anyway. It is a reminder that every fall carries the blueprint for rising, that triumph is often born from fatigue rather than glory. May these words breathe for those who know the weight of doubt yet stand again.

RISE AFTER YOU FALL

On fields of doubt and clover, we stood,
Breathless, yet certain of a coming glory.
Then four leaves rose from the quiet wood,
And promised someone would tell this story.

If there's a tale that must be told,
Let it be of how we rose from the cold,
Not of us hiding in our shells,
But of a comeback where failure once dwelled.

Tell a tale of defeat, not surrender,
Of shields and swords gripped firmly in hand
That swung with weary force when odds were slender,
Of aching knees that still chose to stand.

Let it be a story without pity,
Rejecting the thought of idle compassion.
Instead, let it be marked by triumph's grit,
Wrought by those whose will shapes every action.

A tale that carries a resounding call,
One that will echo, "Rise after you fall!"

What is history if we cannot use it as a reference point? I say this as a reminder: history gives us countless references—moments that prompt action or inaction.

Women and men have abused each other for generations. So commonplace is this cruelty that I have seen it, and you have seen it.

You can wait for gentleness to return,

for someone to choose growth,

for love to remember its promise.

Yet history reminds us through women and men like [insert your victims of choice here]—sadly or perhaps luckily), we have plenty—who endured years of abuse behind closed doors, hoping tenderness would replace cruelty, believing change might one day bloom in the man or woman they once trusted.

But when waiting began to cost pieces of themselves—their voice, their freedom, their joy—they had to walk away with nothing but their name and their will to rise.

Their leaving was not abandonment, but an act of self-preservation—one that taught the world a truth:

Wisdom is found not in holding on, but in choosing when to walk forward without permission.

WAIT

Pair your waiting with a clear contingency,
Not every wait will yield the worth you seek.
Let it guard you from harsh disappointment,
A shield to keep your patience from growing faint.

When I wasn't living the nine-to-five life, I used to look over at that world and think, *Man, they've got a good setup.* Conrad the soldier watched office workers heading home at sunset, briefcase in hand, knowing a warm meal and a soft couch awaited them. They had weekends, office parties, and birthdays in the break room. They laughed by the coffee machine, took lunch in the shade, and went home every day. To me, it looked like stability—routine without danger, comfort without chaos.

But when I finally stepped into that world myself, trading boots for polished shoes and morning formation for morning meetings, I realized there was a whole side of the story I had never seen.

Conrad, the corporate worker, sits under fluorescent lights, heart racing—not from combat drills but from deadlines stacked like sandbags. Emails arrive like rapid fire. Projects pile up. Some days, I stare at my screen so long I forget what the weather outside feels like. People laugh in the break room, yes, but sometimes it's laughter masking burnout. They clock out, carrying work home in their mind like a rucksack with invisible weight.

Funny enough, those same people look back at my time in uniform and think, *He had purpose, structure, brotherhood.* They imagine Conrad the soldier standing tall, certain, disciplined, steady under pressure. They don't see the 4:00 a.m. wakeups, the grit in my teeth, how heat and adrenaline could swallow a man whole. They don't see moments I marched forward, not because I felt brave, but because there was no option to freeze. They don't see the stillness after chaos, when silence rings louder than gunfire.

Two versions of me—same man, different battlegrounds.

Both sides have weight. Both require courage. In each world, I've learned that moving forward doesn't mean becoming a machine. Sometimes progress is slow, sometimes messy. Sometimes the wisest step is not to push harder, but to pause, to breathe, to remember I am human before I am uniformed or employed.

Life isn't a straight march.
It bends, unravels, redirects.
Some days demand movement; others require stillness.
And sometimes, what feels like being late
is exactly the timing we needed.

This is my reminder to myself, and to anyone walking their own winding road: Tread lightly. Move with intention, not automatic rhythm. Because no matter which version of Conrad showed up—the soldier or the corporate worker— both deserve space to simply exist, not just perform.

TREAD LIGHTLY

In an instant
you will see
life is no straight path
but a thread unraveling.

We move forward
without knowing
if the race has a prize.

We sleep and still we breathe,
wandering through dreams
until morning calls us back.

Take each step with care
but do not fear the unknown.
Even familiar roads can lead you astray.

Sometimes the wisest move is to pause.
Sometimes being late is exactly on time.

In the military, death isn't an abstraction; it has a face, a voice you once knew, a bed that suddenly sits empty. I've stood in formation as the "Last Post" echoed across the field, its mournful notes rising into the air, heavy with memory. One moment Private White and I were sharing jokes over cold rations; the next I was staring at a folded flag, wondering how quickly everything can change.

Such moments force reflection. When a comrade falls, you feel your own breath differently—sharper, more precious. You think about how short life can be, how uncertain tomorrow might be. On night watch, during long marches, in quiet rooms where absence speaks louder than words, I've found myself asking, *If it were me, have I lived enough? Loved enough? Left something meaningful behind?*

Grief, painful as it is, brings perspective.
It reminds you to be present.
To value laughter, conversation, and sunlight.
To live deliberately—not later, but now.

LAST POST comes from my loss of a friend and comrade—a loss that sharpened life instead of dulling it. A reminder that facing mortality can awaken gratitude, purpose, and the courage to keep moving forward while we still can. **Rest in power, White "Beige" Horane.**

LAST POST

And when the last post's mournful call was blown,
A quiet wonder stirred within my chest:
Will I be next to rest in Earth's embrace,
Sealed in the stillness of a wooden frame?
This thought brought clarity to fleeting days,
A sharpened sense of life while I still stand.

uch is the mind of those who dared look ahead.
Their minds are unbound by fear, yet deeply aware.
They ponder all that might or might not be,
Exploring every path, each possibility.

The American of options:

We celebrate payday without considering the single mother working two jobs to earn hers. We enjoy a long, hot shower without noticing those who are homeless and facing water restrictions. We bite into fruits from the grocery store, forgetting the hands that picked them under a burning sun.

In our daily routines—coffee runs, commutes, dinners at home—blessings can feel ordinary, even owed. However, somewhere else, someone experiences the same world through a very different lens.

TO EACH HIS OWN is an invitation to look beyond our moment—to ask who else shares it with us, and at what cost. Not from guilt, but from awareness. Not to judge, but to understand. Wisdom grows best when watered with empathy—when we let our view widen just enough to see another perspective standing beside our own.

May these words remind us that blessings are not universal, yet awareness can make us kinder custodians of the abundance we hold.

TO EACH HIS OWN

The sun shines and we smile,
Grateful for the warmth on our skin.
But what about the rivers shrinking?

The rain finally falls, and the farmers rejoice.
But what about those who used the clouds for shade?

The trees stand tall with heavy branches,
Offering fruit, shelter, and shade.
The woodcutter cuts it and calls it a gift.
But what will happen when the forest disappears?

What is given? What is taken?

Seeds for thought, left to take root.

STORIES OF THE STRONG ONE

Her song was like the dreary howl of the wind taking flight.
A mournful hymn that echoes through the void.
Yet woven through the threads of endless night
is hope—her melody cannot be destroyed.

Her song is a shield; her voice is her testament.

"For hell's fierce trials are but tests," she cries,
"And heaven's rest will meet these weary eyes."

I've missed school events for my child and been greeted by disappointed eyes—not angry, just quietly hurt. These are the moments that lingers longer than you expect. I've made promises with the best intentions, only to break them when life outpaced my ability to keep up. Sometimes my efforts fell short, even when my heart was full.

I've failed tests I thought I was prepared for, retaking them with a knot in my stomach and a prayer that this time would be different.

But with time, I've learned this:
Failure isn't proof that we're undeserving—it's proof we're still growing.
It humbles. It sharpens. It leads us inward, then forward.

Every stumble carves a deeper understanding of myself.
Every setback teaches resilience.
Every disappointment makes success more meaningful when it eventually comes.

This is a reminder that failing doesn't disqualify us; it prepares us.
It teaches us to rise again, to try again, and to believe that falling and rising are two parts of the same journey.

FAILURE IS A LESSON

Fail once—like rain that slips through trembling hands.
Fail twice—like waves that crash upon the sand.
Fail again, and let the echoes resound:
Each stumble marks the way where truth is found.

Learn once—from ashes rising in the breeze.
Learn twice—from roots that twist beneath the trees.
Learn again, for every fall holds its place,
A lesson etched in time, a step toward grace.

Failures are seeds, though buried in despair,
They bloom with hope and thrive when given care.
So do not fear the fall; embrace the climb.
Each failure brings you closer over time.

FAILURE

You'll fail, probably more than once.
But if you keep getting up,
if you push through when the path feels impossible,
you'll find success.

Failure makes success meaningful.
They go hand in hand.
Without struggle, victory wouldn't taste so sweet.

CREATOR

When the music fades into quiet air,
Hum the melody—let it linger there.
When the guiding light begins to wane,
Recall each step. The path will remain.

And if the light should vanish from your view,
The strength within will guide you safely through.
Care for yourself; let your heart restore,
Only then can you give or offer more.

If the world forgets to care, stand tall.
Prepared to rise and carry through it all.
When challenges loom—daunting and immense,
It's true—they will ask for all your strength.

Easy trials bring rewards that swiftly fade,
But greater work sees brighter dreams conveyed.
And when the outcome doesn't meet your will,
Create anew. Rise higher, stronger still.

2 UNMASKING ME

If these experiences were left unwritten,
they would rob the world of the bliss that life deserves,
leaving a void in the tapestry of time.
For within the stories of hardship lies perseverance,
a light that inspires the downtrodden to rise again.
Most lives encounter such moments,
but like the blossoms of a mango tree,
some wither, while others bloom into sweet fruit,
fueling the body with energy and joy.
Even fallen blossoms nourish the soil,
yet their potential might soar higher,
exploding into the beauty of fruit.
With this thought, I step into your space,
hoping to be a spark that ignites your energy.
But I am only the spark.
The fire, the fruit, the power—they are within you.
How do you find them?
The answer is simple:
You must be you.

YOU

Hey, you.
yes, you.

not your name,
not your labels,
just you.

Hey, you who stopped reading,
that was your choice.
Do you see your power?

Hey, you who stayed,
curiosity is guiding you,
or maybe you're just wandering.
Both are okay.

Hey, you who smiles,
hold this moment gently.

And you who feels heavy,
let the sadness pass.
There is still room for joy.

Hey, you who resist these words,
try love.
It is lighter to carry.

Hey, you who searches,
keep looking.
The answers will meet you in time.

Hey, you who holds power,
remember its weight.
Use it with care.

Hey, you who feel powerless,
look in the mirror.
Your strength is waiting there.

Hey, you who feel beautiful,
you are learning to love yourself.

And you who feels unseen,
you are still worthy of love.

Hey, you who rushes,
patience will make the journey softer.

Hey, you who doubts,
doubt is a door,
but so is faith.

Hey, you.
It all begins and ends with you.
So…be you.

WHO SHOULD I BE?

I ask myself, who must I be?
A shape that shifts to fit their view?
I chase their love—I beg, I plead,
but in their hands, I cease to be,
a soul unsure of what is true.

I twist and bend to earn their cheer,
perform the part they wish to see.
But in the act, truth disappears,
The mirror shows what I most fear:
a self erased so carefully.

The secret lingers in my chest,
a smile I wear to hide the break.
And those who praise play roles at best,
pretending joy, like all the rest,
while both our hearts begin to ache.

So I become who I am not,
a war I wage inside my mind.
I paint the world the way they thought,
but in my hand, the brush is caught.
Why not let go, why not unwind?

Let watchers cheer—or turn away.
Their fleeting gaze holds little weight.
When I am me, I will not stray.
I'll stand in truth, come what may,
for self is worth the longest wait.

Loyalty is a noble trait—one we're taught to wear like armor. Be faithful. Be dependable. Stand firm.

For a long time, I believed loyalty meant holding on no matter what. To people. To plans. To paths I have outgrown. I've stayed longer than I should have—in friendships that were draining more than nourishing, in commitments that felt like obligation rather than purpose, in goals I pursued simply because they once mattered. It's painful to admit when something we poured our time and heart into is no longer right for us.

We rarely talk about the courage it takes to walk away—not in anger, but in honesty. To look at a path you've followed faithfully and say, "I need a new direction." Sometimes, loyalty means building a bridge that carries you farther. Other times, it means turning around and choosing yourself.

This poem is a reminder that loyalty is powerful, yet it should not chain us to what harms us. The bravest loyalty is often inward—to growth, to truth, to the version of you waiting on the other side of change.

LOYALTY

Be ever wary of where you place your loyalty,
For commitment, though a steadfast consort,
Can betray the trust you place in it.
It is wise to commit to a journey,
But what if that journey leads to a cliff?
You must be ready
To either build a bridge across the divide
Or choose another path toward your destination.
And when you arrive,
If you find that it is not what you expected,
do not pretend that it is.
Admit that the loyalty you gave
was to the wrong cause.
For it is in this honesty that healing begins.
Sometimes the truest loyalty is to yourself,
To the courage it takes to change course,
To reshape your goals,
And to learn from the journey you've walked.

One compliment I often receive is this: "Conrad, you have a way with words. You are good at public speaking." The truth is, it was not always the case. In fact, there was a time when anxiety was all I felt in these kinds of scenarios.

However, the belief that I can do it drowned these anxieties in floods of commitment and practice. I now walk into a room with confidence long before talent arrives.

There were times I stumbled through presentations, voice shaking, notes trembling in my hands—yet I returned the next day, and the day after. Not because I was gifted, but because I refuse to stop believing I belonged there. Over time, the words sharpen. The posture straightens. What once looked like bravery becomes competence—and then mastery.

This poem lives in the space between the confident self you see and the one shaped by discipline into being.

It is neither judgment nor a warning. It is an observation of how belief—or its absence—quietly shapes the lives we end up living. How some paths fade into memory while others leave marks on the world—not through chance, but by conviction.

BELIEVE is about what we choose to hold onto when no one is watching, when applause is absent, when the outcome is uncertain. It is about the quiet decision to keep going—and how, over time, that decision becomes the difference between a story remembered and a life lived.

BELIEVE

Some are born with talent,
But without belief, it fades,
Wasted with time.
In the end, only stories remain,
Tales of a younger self
Told in a regretful tone,
As if to compensate for what could have been.

Others hold their beliefs close,
And from these beliefs, talent is born,
Forged by the will to achieve,
Molded into actions that need no storyteller.

The story unfolds,
Not in whispers of what might have been,
But in the actions that shape the world,
A talent crafted from belief,
A living testament to its maker.

For talent without belief
Fades as swiftly as a shadow at dusk,
While belief breathes life into what seemed impossible,
Transforming potential into reality.

RENDITION OF A SKEPTIC

I see the doubt
in eyes that hide behind the dark:
success—a ghost
that haunts my restless heart.

The whispers creep,
cold and sly,
plotting in silence,
with hearts that lie.

Behind the glass,
they watch with hollow grins.
Their joy is fragile,
built on fear within.

They say, "Turn back,
this is too much,"
but fear is a friend,
if you dare to trust.

For doubt gives birth
to strength to move,
while fear, like risk,
teaches how to improve.

Each tick of time
revives my will,
while dreams take flight
in gray skies still.

So break the chains,
let courage lead,
and build a world
where your dreams are freed.

I AM

I am not the mountain; I am the climb.
I am not reaching; I am the star that shines.
I am not the problem; I am the way.
I paused, not stopped, to rise another day.

I hold the time, for it is never too late
To shape my path, to craft my fate.
I am the spark, the fire, the flame.

This is my truth. This is my name.

PICTURE OF CONFIDENCE

He sat upright, neck firm against his collar,
Every word was sharp, commanding attention.
His eyes, steady, held answers to questions unspoken:
A gaze that dared the world to inquire.

She moved with grace, a quiet storm of power.
Her presence carved space, demanding admiration.
Not once did she falter, her rhythm unbroken;
Each step was a beat of unshakable assurance.

This is the picture of confidence.
Do not merely admire the art.
Step boldly into the frame.
Be the masterpiece.

DIAMONDS

I do not wish to be the diamond's shine,
I want to be the pressure, the design,
The force that carves a splendor yet unseen,
A quiet power shaping what has been.

I'll craft a radiance the world will desire,
A glow so fierce it kindles hearts afire.
I won't wait for destiny to unfold.
I am the maker of the dreams I hold.

Let's revisit the version of Conrad who was very persistent in becoming better at public speaking.

I could have waited for confidence to arrive before speaking.

I could have waited for the right moment, the perfect timing, the ideal version of myself.

What changed was not the fear—but my willingness to move with it. I began asking better questions, not "What if I fail?" but "What if I'm already capable?"

I walked into rooms unsure—voice unsteady, heart racing—and spoke anyway. Not because the anxiety disappeared, but because I learned that waiting, was heavier than acting. Each step forward shrank the excuses. Each attempt turned "someday" into something closer, something tangible.

WHAT IF is about a decision made now. It is not about luck or waiting for perfect timing. It is about action, discipline, and the courage to begin before you feel ready.

An invitation to challenge the stories that hold us back. To test fear instead of obeying it. To recognize that the life we imagine isn't waiting for permission, only movement.

WHAT IF

What if the fear is only in your mind,
And action proves you're good at what you find?
What if there's no lottery, just hard work,
And dreams are built by those who never shirk?

What if you don't wait for the new year's start,
But take the steps now, follow your heart?
What if you say no and stay disciplined,
Choosing health over that fleeting whim?

What if time is enough if you use it right,
And excuses vanish when you step into the light?
What if every goal moves you forward, true,
When someday becomes the day you break through?

What if someday is today?

LEGACY

When you transcend to the other side,
What impact will you leave behind?
What will your legacy be?
If you don't know, perhaps you've yet to dream.

If the answer is "nothing,"
What a wasted life that would be.

Leave a very lasting mark,
Or strive to leave the world better than you found it.

Make your legacy so positive,
That your name endures.

Never save the best for last.
Approach each task with your fullest effort.

Then, when you transcend,
You'll do so without regret.

If you can, read MY VOICE aloud—especially if you are by yourself.

This short piece is not just an expression—it is a release.
Not just courage—but care.
A reminder that speaking up doesn't just change the room.
It changes the body.
And sometimes, it changes a life.

MY VOICE

My voice is no longer muted or weak.
It rises loudly to firmly take a stand
For those who were shamed when they dared to speak
And stories once buried by silencing hands.

My voice—a megaphone, a rising tide,
Declaring, "I'll be heard," refusing to hide.

ALLOWANCE

"You cannot," they said.
A knife cuts deep, but it shapes.
I choose to create.

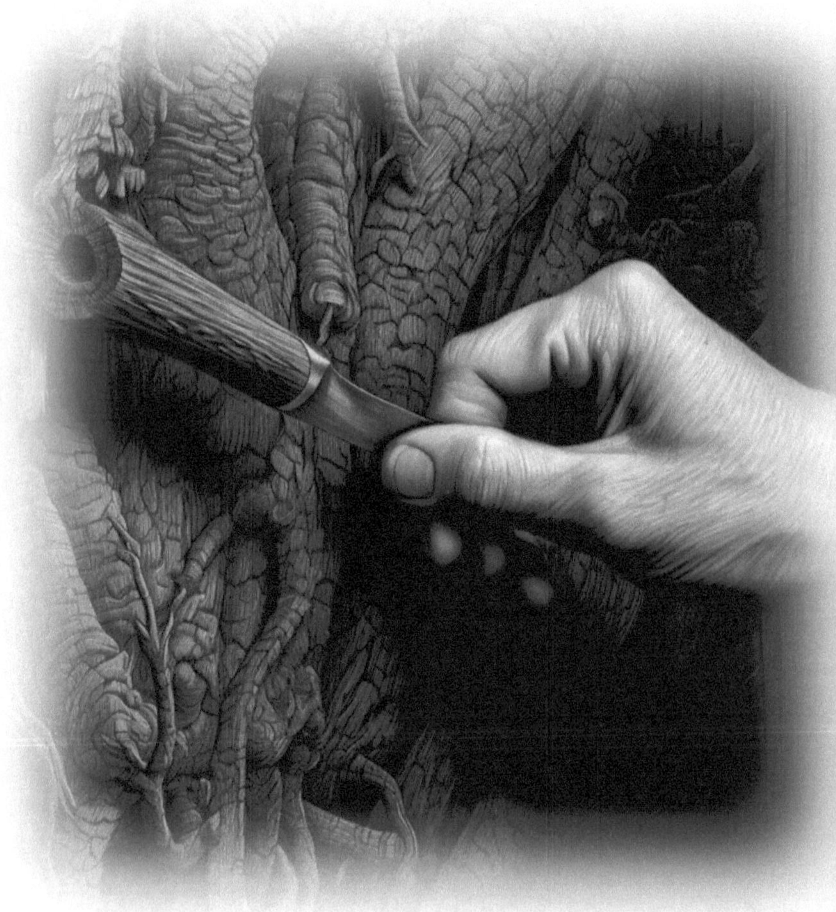

"You cannot," they said.
A knife cuts deep, but it shapes.
I choose to create.

REFLECTION

Today I faced my greatest foe,
A shadowed self I'd come to know.
Through honest words, we made a pact,
A bond unbroken, ever intact.

The mirror holds our fiercest fight,
Yet spurs the soul to take its flight.
So meet yourself with an open embrace,
A friend within your truest space.

STRONG

You are strong,
Though weakness may have overtaken you.
Strength will be your companion once more.
Let this moment be the start of your reunion.

As you read *The Journey to Now,* something will begin to shift.

You will find yourself sharing the inspiration gained from these pages—in conversation, in reflection, sometimes without even realizing it. Inevitably, some will scoff. If not with words, then with a look—a pause, a raised eyebrow that silently asks, "You got all that from reading one book?"

Do not let that moment derail your journey.

I have felt the weight of shame in those spaces—the subtle pressure to downplay growth, shrink insight, soften conviction so others feel more comfortable. Shame has a way of disguising itself as realism, humility, or "not taking things too seriously." But often, it is simply fear of change wearing a familiar face.

Growth is rarely loud. It does not always announce itself with certainty or proof. Sometimes it begins quietly—with a line that lingers, a thought that challenges, a reflection that refuses to let you return to who you were. That is not exaggeration. That is awakening.

If this book gives you language for something you have long felt but never named, trust it. If it sharpens your awareness or strengthens resolve, honor it. Insight does not need permission to be valid, and transformation does not need consensus to be real.

SHAME ME AGAIN

Oh, shame, you come with words sharp as stone,
Seeking to break, to bend, to crush my soul.
Yet your heavy weight is but an incentive,
A spark that stirs the fire within me whole.

You wrap your grasp around my fragile mind,
But like Teflon, your grip cannot take hold.
With every whisper, I grow more refined,
Inventing strength from what your doubts unfold.

I am not moved when you declare my fall,
Nor does your pity haunt my restless nights.
For in your seeds, I find the power to call
Reason from the depths and take new flights.

You will not rule the life I choose to lead.
Though I must face you, I will not give in.
You fuel the courage that I truly need
To rise and prove the strength I've found within.

Shame, you mark the path I must now walk,
But you are the spark that lights my way.
You, who seek to silence me with talk,
Are the very reason I find strength today.

PENS

My friend will tell me what I want to hear;
My foe will tell me what I don't.
Both speak from bias: one from love,
The other from a place of disdain.

When doubt creeps in, I trust my pen:
It will not lie nor lead me astray.
It points me true, without hesitation,
An arrow guiding me toward my aim.

TO BE AN ALPHA

A status coveted by many,
But achieved by only a few.
Look closely, and you'll find the alpha
In places most unexpected.
An alpha does not wave a weapon,
But carries it with quiet strength.
Versatile in its use,
You'll never see it
Until the time calls for it.
The alpha has emotions,
But they're constantly in check;
Mastered, never held on a leash.
He is not the loudest,
Yet commands attention with calm.
Though she hurts,
She seeks the remedy to her pain.
He is dangerous, yet harmless,
A warrior, yet peaceful,
Knowledgeable, yet always a student,
Confident, yet listening,
Happy to live, no matter the day or circumstance.
With his structure, time is limitless,
Yet to the onlooker, it seems he has none.
She keeps her goals quiet,
But they strike like the sunrise:
Achievements are visible without warning.
The alpha's roots begin in the mind,
Guiding emotions to rise or remain suppressed.

Not everyone will be an alpha,
But striving to be one is a worthwhile goal.

LIONS

You are a lion—
Your roar distinct,
Your actions command attention.
You lead your pride,
But leadership must be earned.

Ambitions to become a pilot—failed.
Ambitions to become an army officer—failed.
Ambitions to become the best soldier—passed.
Ambitions to become an Author—passed.
Ambitions to become a business owner—passed;

Same person, different task, many lessons, same focus. Only the best efforts are good enough.

All these apply to me. Yet I understood that in every task, a learning experience awaits.

That belief has guided me more than any outcome ever could. It reminds me that effort is never wasted—even when results fall short of what I imagined. Every attempt carries insight. Every failure teaches. Every step forward, no matter how small, leaves one stronger than before.

Approaching a task with your best effort does not mean perfection. It means presence. It means showing up fully, knowing that growth happens in the act of trying, not just in the result. Too often, we measure ourselves against impossible standards and forget that progress begins with participation.

This poem exists in that understanding.

ATTEMPT is not about becoming the best in the world. It is about choosing a direction that moves you forward. It is about honoring the courage to begin, to learn, and to continue—even without certainty. Because the best version of yourself is not the one who never falls short, but the one who keeps trying with intention.

In every attempt, there is becoming.

ATTEMPT

Will I become the best in the world?
Perhaps not—
But let this be my target.
The best version of myself
Is one who dares to try.

FAIL WELL

Failure lights the path,
whispers secrets to the bold.
Rise and chase the fire.

SET FREE

I saw them there so closely packed,
Their brilliance glimmered in the sky.
Yet only when their chains were cracked,
Did they ascend and learn to fly.

And there they went for all to see,
Dreams of every size and shape.
Like caged-up birds now flying free,
Rejoicing in their grand escape.

But some remained and would not soar,
As if they sought a guiding light.
Their owners left and locked the door,
Abandoning their dreams to night.

Yet mine was smiling back at me,
As if to say, "You hold my key."

I reached to open what was sealed,
Its spark ignited, burning bright.
A boundless power was revealed,
As it ascended into flight.

It soared ahead to lead my way,
And chart a path for me to see.
Its brilliance painted night as day,
Unlocking my own destiny.

It joined with others, dreams aligned,
The grandest vision ever seen.
To think they once were so confined,
In minds and thoughts, and in between.

Now nevermore will they go back,
To places where their freedoms lack.

3 ECHOES OF PURPOSE

As a soldier, I learned early that good intentions do not always bring comfort.

There were moments when I stood in full camouflage, tasked with protection, yet saw fear—not relief—reflected back at me. The very uniform meant to signal safety carried the weight of threat for those who did not know my purpose. I wanted to help. I was trained to help. Yet my presence alone unsettled those I was meant to protect. That contradiction lingered.

It taught me a lesson I did not expect.

Strength can protect, but it can also overwhelm. Even wisdom, when delivered without awareness, can miss its mark. I've seen how easily capability is mistaken for appropriateness, assuming that what works in one setting must work everywhere.

This poem lives in that recognition.

USES is not a rejection of skill, strength, or survival. It is a reminder that purpose depends on placement. That what sustains one path may disrupt another. True understanding requires us to pause, observe, and ask not only, "What can I offer?" but "Is this what is needed here?"

It is an invitation to humility—and discernment—in how we move through the lives of others.

USES

Petrol flows—a liquid with purpose,
But not one to quench thirst.
A flame sparks brilliance,
Yet the owl prefers the cover of night.

The hunter survives by taking life,
Needing destruction to keep living.
Death—so inevitable and near,
Yet it finds us mostly unprepared.

Your skills may fit your journey
But not the paths of others.

REGRET

Dreams left unfulfilled
Met him beyond the grave's door.
Tears of regret fall.

PROGRESSION

If everyone were content with their lives,
The world would remain stagnant, frozen in time.

Progression thrives on discomfort,
On differing views,
Not in opposition but in necessary contrast.

Your perspective is not foolish,
It's the spark that ignites change,
Building bridges toward a progressive future.

So, bring your voice to the table.
Your idea might be the step we need to take to move forward.

Grades, titles, reviews, and projections—all measurements that are acceptable when measured by oneself. However, if numbers and opinions are offered as conclusions rather than guesses, the damage can be irreversible.

I know this—I've felt the pull of those measurements, the subtle pressure to let someone else's confidence or doubt stand in for my own judgment. It is easy to forget how quickly external voices can start to sound like truth when repeated often enough.

But I've learned that predictions are not outcomes.

People will tell you who you are capable of being—sometimes generously, sometimes carelessly. Yet none of these assessments account for the variable that matters most: the choices you make when no one is watching, the effort you give when certainty is absent, the resolve you carry when belief wavers.

This serves as motivation to resist outsourcing authorship. It acknowledges that success and failure are not fixed states handed down by opinion—they are results shaped by intention and action. It is a reminder that while others may offer their calculations, only you decide which inputs matter.

You are not the sum of someone else's math.
You are the equation's turning point.

BEST OF ENEMIES

Turn your "ifs" into actions,
step after step, until dreams
are no longer distant.

Regret will meet you,
not as a foe to crush,
but as a shadow at your back,
urging you toward the light.

It whispers of missed chances,
not to haunt,
but to remind you
that growth comes from daring
and discomfort births strength.

Regret is not your downfall,
but the best of enemies,
challenging you to rise.

QUANTIFY

They can say I will fail.
They can say I will succeed.
But their words mean nothing,
empty and weightless,
until I choose to give them power.

I am the fulcrum—
the balance that tips
between success and failure.

No prophecy defines me.
No opinion controls my fate.
The outcome is mine to shape.

I am the most vital variable
in the equation of my life.

HERE OR THERE

I climbed.
All I found was the empty wind
whispering promises that weren't mine.

I turned back,
and there it was, where I had stood,
waiting quietly in the shadow of my steps.

I only needed to root myself,
to see the worth of my space,
the value of my time,
and the dream already blooming within me.

SUCCESS

When I was a child,
I reached for the horizon of adulthood.
When I became an adult,
I longed for the simple lines of a stickman.

When I was hungry,
I dreamed of feasts.
When the feast arrived,
it weighed me down with discomfort.

When I was single,
I envisioned the warmth of marriage.
When I was married,
I glanced back at the freedom of solitude.

In war, I cried for peace.
In peace, I vowed to fight to protect it.

Desires shift like sand in the wind.
Be careful how you measure success.

During my transition from soldier to corporate professional:

In uniform, expectations were explicit. Structure was clear. Questions were encouraged—clarity meant safety and efficiency. But in the corporate world, I found myself hesitating. Simple office norms—how to word an email, when to follow up, who actually owned a decision—felt strangely unfamiliar. I watched, guessed, and overthought. Tasks that should have taken minutes often took hours—not because the work was difficult, but because I tried to figure them out silently.

Eventually, I began asking.

Not perfectly. Not confidently every time. But honestly. And something shifted. The mystery dissolved. Processes clarified. Relationships strengthened. Tasks that once drained energy became efficient—even simple. What changed wasn't my capability; it was my willingness to seek clarity rather than sit with uncertainty.

From that realization, this piece was born.

Asking does not make us less competent. It makes us more effective. And while the answer may not always be what we hope for, it gives us the grounding we need to move forward—no longer guessing, no longer stalled, no longer lost.

TO KNOW

What if I ask,
and the answer is no?
At least the mystery fades.

If I never ask,
I stay lost in doubt,
unmoored,
never knowing where the truth resides.

So I will ask,
even if the answer is no,
at least now I know.

THE WAY WE MUST LIVE

Don't dwell on things beyond your control.
Such worry weighs your mind in vain.
Focus on what you can tend to now,
And break free from that inner strain.

Be a master of the tasks you hold,
A guide who leads with calm intent.
Take advice with an open ear,
But choose what serves your heart's intent.

Absorb the knowledge in your path,
And seek it out when it's not near.
What you don't need in this moment's grasp
Will find its use when the time is clear.

Let pain pass swiftly as it comes,
And hold on to joy as long as you can.
Hoarding pain makes the mind grow dull,
But happiness sharpens your plan.

Live as if the world's a playground bright,
Where others seek their fleeting bliss.
Live with morals, a steady guide,
And let your conscience lead you through this.

WE WERE HERE

It was not the hope that killed me,
but it kept me lingering at doorsteps, worn smooth by waiting.

It made me believe in apologies shaped from silence
in the hand that reached but never held.
It made me fragile, like the missing edge of a Jenga stack.

The inevitability of it all.

Is it the hope that kills you?

Or is it the waiting, the yearning,
the not knowing when to let it go?

PLACES

The place you come from—
whether in mind or body,
will not dictate the path ahead.

The place where you stand now—
this moment,
is the one within your control.
Put your best effort into it,
and it will help heal the past,
shape the future,
and create the life you seek.

Your present moment
is the one that matters most.

EMBRACE

When hardship comes, it one day will arrive,
Embrace it like a friend you've come to know.
Accept it with grace, for through it we thrive,
A step toward the strength you long to show.

When disappointment knocks, meet it with peace,
Not in joy, but in knowing it must pass.
Through every trial, let your doubts release,
And watch the broken willow grow at last.

When pain has you down, pinned to the floor,
Endure the storm and never lose your stance.
For pity and despair serve you no more;
You must stand strong if you are to advance.

Wait for the moment to strike with the right fist;
Channel your pain, and you will not miss.

I came from a place where life moved at a steady pace, and effort had a clear purpose. Over time, that life gave way to new environments: first the city, then the military, and eventually a foreign country. Each transition brought not only growth and opportunity, but also distance from the simplicity that once grounded me.

As life grew more complex, so did the pressure. In structured systems and spaces of high expectation, I learned discipline, resilience, and focus. Yet when the demands of the corporate world intensify, I sometimes find myself thinking back to the life I lived before everything became measured, urgent, and scrutinized.

Not because I want to undo the journey, but because that earlier life reminds me of who I am when the noise falls away.

This poem lives in that quiet pull.

It reflects the tension between moving forward and turning inward—the understanding that even as we evolve, parts of us remain anchored to where our values first took root. It reflects on progress, memory, and the places we carry long after we have left them behind.

HOMEWARD BOUND

'Tis that longing for the home I once knew,
The creaking hinges on wooden gates
Urged by the cool mountain breeze that blew
Meeting just right, like the best of mates.

The nightly orchestra of chirping bugs
That formed a band by morning's light
Has vanished now: no sound, no thuds,
No whispered song, no band in sight.

And oh, the planting and the reaping,
A satisfaction like no other.
To sow and toil while the world is sleeping,
Bound to the land, just like a mother.

A son must heed his mother's call,
Embracing the gust of a homeward breeze.
For this is home, though not for all.
So I return to my broad-leaf trees.

My squeaky gate, I'll be with you soon.
Prepare your embrace at the next full moon.

THE EARLY FARMER

The farmer sleeps by six-thirty each night,
Then wakes before the sun begins to rise.
At first sight, he greets the breaking light,
As dawn spills softly across the skies.

He passes the rooster, heading for perch,
It greets him with a glance that seems to say,
"Once more, you've come, though I've yet to search
For the horn that signals the break of day."

His boots and the dew are companions true,
The soil stirs gently with a whispered sigh,
"You again?" but they both already knew,
That he'd be there before the sun was high

Early to bed, and early to reap,
For him the dawn is not for rest or sleep.

THE FARMER'S HAT

Whose hat is this, all torn and dirt-stained
Sitting next to the brown wooden chair?
It rests like a symbol of toil sustained,
A silent sentinel waiting there.

As I approached, the tension did rise.
Its stillness seemed to hold a quiet threat.
A stranger might falter, filled with surprise,
Its purpose a mystery, a lingering bet.

Whatever its role, it waits by the door,
Stationed firm beside the man asleep.
Lying in wait, guarding evermore,
If not for the gate, I might not have peeped.

But suddenly, a hand moved and reached out
And brushed it gently as a best friend would.
Now it is clear—it's his, there's no doubt.
It became his crown as he slowly stood.

To him, there is no tear. The stains aren't a lot.
To them, each other is all they have got.

Before I learned what bravery was meant to look like, I felt it beside me.

I was a boy living on a farm, still finding my place in the world, when Savage entered my life. He wasn't human, yet his presence made me feel stronger than I could explain. With him nearby, fear felt smaller. The unknown felt manageable. I walked a little taller simply because he walked beside me.

We often believe that positive energy must come from people—from encouragement, approval, or shared understanding. However, sometimes that energy exists beyond human interaction. Sometimes it exists in loyalty without words, in presence without judgment, in a steady companion who asks nothing of you but simply to be.

Savage carried that kind of energy. He didn't inspire courage through instruction; he inspired it through consistency. Simply by being there. His quiet watchfulness made space for confidence to grow, long before I knew how to create it on my own.

DOGS is not just admiration for animals, but recognition of the ways they shape us. A bond without language can still inspire strength, hope, and resolve. Savage reminded me that courage doesn't always roar; it sometimes sits patiently at your side, offering belief before you've learned to find it yourself.

DOGS

Undoubtedly, dogs are superheroes,
Or maybe they're gods in disguise, unknown.
Their loyalty revealed when care is shown,
Fealty given with no need to impose.

How do they give hope by just existing,
Mending hearts with nothing but a bark?
When you give up, they keep on insisting,
Igniting light in the depths of the dark.

And how could they just patiently wait,
Watching the entrance with curious ears?
Euphoria increases when you are late,
As if you were gone for thousands of years.

To enhance life void of judgment or questions,
Superheroes or gods are my suggestions.

As I mentioned, my journey to this point did not begin with abundance or advantage.

Two central pieces helped shape the Conrad I am today.

My early years were shaped by effort, patience, and the quiet presence of my grandparents. They were not armed with titles, degrees, or formal education, but what they lacked in credentials they carried in wisdom. A wisdom earned through living, observing, enduring, and loving without condition.

They were a constant light.

When I was unsure, they did not overwhelm me with answers. They listened. They offered guidance in simple words that stayed with me long after the conversations ended. Their advice never felt rehearsed or complicated; it felt right. It came from experience, not theory, and guided me more reliably than any instruction manual ever could.

As I moved toward adulthood, their influence became a compass. They helped me see beyond immediate struggle, fear, and limitation. Even when they didn't fully understand the world I was entering, they understood that there were certain values I needed to face what lay ahead—and that understanding was enough to keep me on a path toward growth and success.

This poem was born from that gratitude.

GRANDPARENTS COME FROM HEAVEN is not about idealizing the past but about honoring the quiet power of those who guide us with love and lived wisdom. Those who shape our lives not by what they know academically, but by what they have come to understand about character, resilience, and the kind of strength that carries us forward long after their words have been spoken.

GRANDPARENTS COME FROM HEAVEN

I'm sure grandparents leave their homes at night
To visit realms where grandkids cannot tread.
How else do they make everything feel right,
Or heal the silent hurts we've left unsaid?

They lift our masks with wisdom's gentle hand,
And offer guidance from their boundless graces.
They plant solutions like seeds in the sand,
To bloom and bring a smile upon our faces.

Their hugs are where the truest warmth resides,
Each pat affirms, "You've got this. Don't let go."
Their comfort strengthens as our doubt subsides,
Transforming fear into a steady glow.

At dusk, they stretch the hours just for you,
To steal the light before the day is done.
They guard your dreams until the morning's hue,
Protecting you until the night is won.

They won't depart until their work is clear,
Their lessons etched within the heart they guide.
Only then do they rise and disappear,
With faith that you will walk your path with pride.

The men who're eighty, yet are still just seven;
I'm sure their secret place must be in heaven.

A RIVER OF POTENTIAL

How did you begin your success?
I reached for the river of potential—
its waters clear, shimmering with promise.

With unsteady hands,
I dipped my cup
and began to drink.

Each sip quenched a thirst
I hadn't known was so vast,
filling me with the will to achieve.

I will share a reminder that my grandparents gave me before they departed. This advice proves to be applicable now more than ever. They spoke of balance: doing what needed to be done when it needed to be done, and resting when the body asked for it.

As I grew older, I drifted further from those beginnings. The world grew louder. Time became something to manage instead of something to respect. Schedules replaced signals, and progress began to feel like pressure. I learned how easily we ignore our own needs in the pursuit of achievement, forgetting that discipline without awareness eventually costs more than it gives.

This poem embodies a return to what matters.

It is a reminder that structure should serve growth, not silence it, and that honoring necessity is often the most disciplined choice we can make.

NECESSITIES

Sleep when your body calls for rest,
Not when the clock dictates your needs.
Eat when hunger stirs within you,
Not when the hour marks its lead.

Act because it is necessary:
For growth, for change, for something more.
Your schedule is only valuable
when it serves the path you're meant to explore.

From the outside, success often appears effortless.

I remember standing in Times Square, watching a street magician work a deck of cards. Surrounded by noise, lights, and passing crowds, he held everyone's attention with ease. Cards appeared, vanished, changed places. The audience laughed, gasped, and applauded. To most onlookers, it felt spontaneous—pure luck, quick hands, a bit of charm.

But as I watched more closely, I noticed something else.

Every movement was intentional. Every pause deliberate. The trick didn't begin when the card was revealed; it began long before anyone was watching. What looked like magic was actually preparation, practice, and precision unfolding exactly as planned.

I liken success to the sleight of hand I witnessed that day.

THE MAGIC THAT IS YOU is a reminder not to be fooled by appearances, or to remain an onlooker impressed by outcomes without understanding the process behind them. Behind every moment that looks like chance is a carefully crafted plan, rehearsed in private and executed with purpose.

Rather than waiting to be amazed by the results of others, this poem invites you to step behind the curtain. To study the craft. To plan deliberately. To practice patiently. And to recognize that the magic you admire is not a coincidence but the result of intention, effort, and mastery at work.

THE MAGIC THAT IS YOU

Success is magic, with the world your stage,
A craft of wonder, hidden yet profound.
But no illusion shines without the mage;
It takes your effort to make it astound.

A rabbit drawn from shadows stirs delight,
Its leap a plan, unseen but well-prepared.
To passive eyes, it's shrouded in the night,
But action weaves the threads of what's declared.

It's the royal cards tucked within the deck,
Held firm until the moment calls their play.
With steady hands, you guard them from the wreck,
And shape the outcome, bold, in your own way.

Success is a coin that spins in the air,
Its face unknown, yet yours to oversee.
You tip the scales with faith, focus, and care,
For magic is your will—and mastery.

Each flip invites a chance to redefine
Where effort makes the magic truly shine.

4 BECOMING

When I first began writing my thoughts in a notebook, it wasn't with an audience in mind.

I wrote because I was curious—curious about my own thinking, and just as curious about the inner worlds of others. I wanted to understand how people make sense of their lives, their fears, their hopes. Somewhere along the way, I knew I wanted to share those thoughts openly, the same way I'm drawn to the honest reflections of others.

It turns out that desire is far from unique.

Studies and publishing estimates suggest that nearly 80 percent of adults want to write a book, yet only about 3 percent ever finish a draft, and fewer than 1 percent see their work published. Not because most people lack ideas or depth, but because life intervenes. Because perfectionism stalls momentum. Because not knowing where to start becomes a reason not to begin at all.

I recognized myself in this statistic. The question becomes, which group will I be a part of?

There came a moment when avoidance lost its disguise. I had explanations that sounded responsible, delays that felt justified, and reasons that had followed me since youth. They were convincing, familiar even—but familiarity does not make them true.

What changed was not my circumstance, but honesty.

I realized the obstacle I kept naming had slowly taken my shape. Not as failure, but as hesitation. Not as inability, but as permission to wait. And once I could see it clearly, the illusion lost its power.

TODAY'S EXCUSE IS ME is about taking ownership. It marks the moment when responsibility becomes freedom, when the choice to act replaces the comfort of delay. It is about standing fully present, willing to begin, and accepting the role of creator rather than observer.

Because transformation does not start with perfect conditions.

It starts the day we stop pretending we are not ready.

TODAY'S EXCUSE IS ME

Today, again, I faced the illusion
Trying to convince me it held the truth.
With master strokes, it painted the delusion,
A picture carried since the days of youth.

But today, my gaze remains unflinching:
Eyes forward, fixed with resolve set ablaze.
Hands reborn stretch outward, ever reaching,
Ready to discard those disappointing days.

This moment ushers in a time to transform,
To clear the slate, a canvas pure and bare:
Prepared, at last, for the artist to reform
And shape a vision etched beyond despair.

Today, I rise, the artist of my view.
Today, I act, creating something new.

MOTIVATE DISCIPLINE

Motivation is for everyone—easily spoken about
But not discipline—this is earned.
Motivation without discipline is empty.

FOR THE DISCIPLINED

Yes, it is hard,
Yes, it takes time,
Yes, you might fail,
Yes, you will have success,
But none of it comes without discipline.

If it were easy,
Everyone would do it,
And it would lose its worth.

So take on the habit.
Show up every day,
Even when you don't feel like it.
Fail again and again,
But keep going—
Until the results start to show.

DREAMER

How big should I dream?
Think as though you'll achieve what no one else has.
In daring to dream,
You begin to make it real.

DREAMS

You are an ambush waiting to pounce upon your dreams.
If you fall asleep, your dreams will pass by without ever
springing the trap.

There is a truth that we must accept: Yesterday is gone, tomorrow is unknown, and today is what we have. As such, the best decision you can make is to act upon the lessons you have learned from yesterday and apply them today so that you will give tomorrow its best potential.

DREAMS ARE JUST DREAMS

If you can start with a single thought,
You've done more than a doubter ever sought.
For the doubter's words are filled with delay.
"I would," "I should," "I could," they always say.

But action is the key to breaking free,
While doubt locks you away from what could be.
Promises fade without the will to act,
Leaving dreams hollow, lost in empty fact.

A dream not acted upon holds no worth,
Like promises of water in the dirt.
It's only through doing, despite the fear,
That success begins to draw near.

A dream not started remains a wish,
Fading like the morning mist.
"I could" and "I should" are not enough—
Act now, or life will call your bluff.

A LOVELY PAIN

Love should not bring pain—
Chaos disguised as passion.
Rise and set it free.

A FAR-FETCHED LOVE

Love—so deep, yet always out of reach.
We would rather leave our flaws unseen than say, "I am wrong."
It feels like a dream—so fragile, yet so true.
But love takes time, and that starts with you.

Just as a farmer and the earth come together to create life, you, too, possess the power to harness an energy that drives your existence. I share this energy with you now—not as a fleeting spark, but as a lasting force. Let this moment of motivation ignite something deeper within.

Remember this: The energy you invest shapes the outcome. It's not just about fleeting enthusiasm; it's about consistently directing your focus, learning from every experience, and transforming setbacks into growth.

In every task, there's a lesson waiting to be discovered. Hold on to the positives, learn from the negatives, and turn both into fuel for your continuous rebirth. Through this constant renewal, you will find the strength to become the best version of yourself.

ABOUT THE AUTHOR

Conrad Wallace is a country boy at heart, with a deep love for the outdoors and the quiet inspiration it offers. Whether surrounded by open fields or beneath a canopy of trees, he finds creativity in the world around him. A true admirer of art history, Conrad is drawn to curations that tell a story, and his passion for illustration is evident through his carefully selected works.

Beyond his love for the outdoors, Conrad is also a dedicated writer. His children's book, *Your Wonderful Face*, is a heartfelt celebration of confidence and inclusivity, a perfect introduction for young readers who are learning to embrace themselves and others.

With a pen in hand and an appreciation for the beauty of both words and images, Conrad Wallace continues to craft stories that inspire and uplift.

You can learn more about Conrad and his work at conradwallaceauthor.com